[image description:

rhomboids seethe on an indigo background.
what fifteen minutes looks like: on a clouded
day, paper offcuts from a blade. to dislodge

one's mind from thought is a repetitive effort
like my arm wielding an exit shaped like silver
light or reaching for you. I touched the logic

of empire signing my name to an arts council.
yes cyanotype yes enfoldment yes unknowing
what this country does. listening is a form of touch.

touch a negotiation of power. during the Cold War
the CIA funded writers as diplomats. sliced pages
sonic motion. is a poem a machine and built for

illustration or instruction? to score is both a noun
and a verb, notch the surface. victory or defeat
measured as a contingent property of an action.

on an overnight flight, what's gone fades
into a single point on the horizon. absence
is not emptiness, it aches. it fills with aching

like a flock of birds lifting a fishing net into
the blue aching air. a haunting of context.
François Tosquelles wrote, *Psychoanalysis is*

characterized by a requirement to invent. Frantz Fanon
declared total integration an impossibility. a psychiatry

that transforms is one that moves toward self-

destruction. inside the cocoon the caterpillar
digests its own body. the hospital inverts
the world, a negative space in one's personal

history. in the sound of nothing, the poet hears
DESTROY THE ASYLUM brick by brick, the sky
pouring out in all directions. wind scatters shadow

across the fabric. blue an ink that cannot be erased.
if to listen is to enter time's interior. whatever loss
has touched, light's hands touched first.]

MADNESS BELONGS TO THE PEOPLE

JODY CHAN

Brick Books
Prince Edward County, Ontario

Library and Archives Canada Cataloguing in Publication

Title: Madness belongs to the people / Jody Chan.
Names: Chan, Jody, author.
Identifiers: Canadiana (print) 20260187720 | Canadiana (ebook) 20260187739
ISBN 9781771316828 (softcover) | ISBN 9781771316835 (EPUB) | ISBN 9781771316842 (PDF)
Subjects: LCGFT: Poetry.
Classification: LCC PS8605.H3549 M33 2026 | DDC C811/.6—dc23

We gratefully acknowledge the Canada Council for the Arts, the Government of Canada through the Canada Book Fund, and the Ontario Arts Council and the Government of Ontario for their support of our publishing program.

Canada Council for the Arts | Conseil des Arts du Canada

ONTARIO ARTS COUNCIL
CONSEIL DES ARTS DE L'ONTARIO

With the participation of the Government of Canada
Avec la participation du gouvernement du Canada | Canada

Edited by Cecily Nicholson.
Author photo by Albert Hoang.
The book is set in Dante MT.
Cover design by Michael DeForge.
Inside cover by Myung-Sun Kim.
Design by Greg Tabor.

BRICK BOOKS
poetry's home

CERTIFIED CANADIAN PUBLISHER

www.brickbooks.ca

Though much of the work of Brick Books takes place on the ancestral lands of the Anishinaabeg, Haudenosaunee, Huron-Wendat, and Mississaugas of the Credit peoples, our editors, authors, and readers from many backgrounds are situated from coast to coast to coast in Canada on the traditional and unceded territories of over six hundred nations who have cared for Turtle Island from time immemorial. While living and working on these lands, we are committed to hearing and returning the rightful imaginative space to the poetries, songs, and stories that have been untold, under-told, wrongly told, and suppressed through colonization.

The madness of revolution is to burn in its oven day by day.
We bestow it our entire lives, not merely the hours of our days.

WISAM RAFEEDIE, *THE TRINITY OF FUNDAMENTALS*

The time for talking has ended, the time for acting has begun.

FRANTZ FANON, *THE WRETCHED OF THE EARTH*

TABLE OF CONTENTS

MOVEMENT III

MOVEMENT IV

MOVEMENT V

TRACKLIST

MOVEMENT I

MOVEMENT II

MOVEMENT III

MOVEMENT IV

MOVEMENT V

[performance score:

scan the code to access five tracks. the invitation is to listen to each piece of music alongside its corresponding movement in the text. if you reach the end of the text before the music, keep reading, or notice the absence of sound. if you reach the end of the music before the text, keep listening, or move on.

there is no wrong way to be here.

the work is yours now.]

MOVEMENT I

[audio score:

woodblock drips. snap of clocks. snare
drum surface sing, frenzied song of block
and chain and metronome ticks out fours.
ring of dinner ready, drive-through latch
snapping open and shut. woodblock bends
the distance between seconds, sound
stretched over a frame. the gravity of even
count. where once you heard the cymbal
sing, dream house inside out, what luck when the performance

does not take place on this page, when the poem contacts not

a square of sanity, not one. madness describes
an energetic state. I grasp onto objects as allies

in materiality. organ (electric), time (manual):
tuition for art therapy, add to cart.

It's like we're holding hands now at the edge of a white
silence, from which we are to make a music
of our being here, of being moved (Taylor Johnson)

the wilderness was all
around me, rupturing my histories—

1953: Jean Oury buys the castle La Borde. rampant his drive
for reflection, to analyze that idea of asylum
which occurs definitionally and that which becomes

a portal. Félix Guattari devises a grid to randomize
responsibility, then the patient creates   herself:

Psychosis shows its true face only in
a collective life developed around it

sounds are inherently shadows of vibration, relationship
an instrument of resonance, not restraint
nor electroshock insulin nor confinement in a square   alone.

to move is to make a mark with the body.
what you and I hear depends on where you are
in the room, depends on who I is

this I is you
this I is I

language mediates encounters of the subject (listened-to)
object (listening) verb (time) body (music). does not
draw blood.   patients walk and walk
and nurses wash the dishes.

care is also a confrontation
square ( ) home ( ) cell
mind ( ) organ ( ) space

listening to land is not a pristine act (Dylan Robinson)

A poem is not the finger on the trigger of a resistance fighter's gun
(Jamila Osman)

]

GENESIS

half human, half fish. peaches
　　　　sweetened when squeezed in a fist

the difference between fact
　　　　and fiction is the calibre of storytelling

outcast, monster, dissonance, rebel. I
　　　　conjured a wildness. a wall

of muffled sound, for shelter. not everyone's
　　　　mothers hunt them in their sleep

I was a child. I mimicked every night-
　　　　mare. first, the splinter. then

the rot. if you love me, I bruise,
　　　　the way sugar pools under pressure

before, I was a larva, halved
　　　　by terror. I told a student therapist

about my mother's anger. received their face
　　　　as echo, prescient, before I could be angry

myself. inside, a fragment of dissent: marked
　　　　feral; a pit, knotted and poisonous, sinking

through the water

SONOGRAM

sound, as in

vibration, the residue of words
patterns of resonance in the skin

drumhead, fish scale
or regulatory membrane

undamaged, uncompromised, based
on logic, sense, or reason

echo, as in

the meaning delivered after delay

history reflecting off a wall
or another hard surface

a tail, clapping water
a mother, slapping

privacy screen, medical bill
the bottom of a well

what one perceives most clearly in an empty room

sound the origin of echo
echo the endpoint of absence
I I I I reading into a blue gap
reaching out of a cellular silence

ECHOLALIA

Don don ko doko doko. Don don ko doko doko! Taiko repertoire is often taught orally, relying on repetition. I learn to drum through kuchi shōga, a system of call-and-response phonetic notation. The body learns first, then the mind follows. Vibrations felt in our feet, in our instruments' round faces. In the streets, too, I'll follow any megaphone: I believe that we will win, I chant obediently, even when I don't. Without context, can language be trusted? Can sound?

( )

Echolalia, in medical parlance, is pathologized and stigmatized as a meaningless repetition. In *The Future Is Disabled,* Leah Lakshmi Piepzna-Samarasinha describes echolalia instead as a language that doctors have not made the effort to understand.

( )

Kuchi shōga is both fixed and unfixed, contextual and shared. Many of its onomatopoeic syllables signify universally. But different groups, or even pieces, can curate their own idiosyncratic set of sounds, corresponding to a left- or right-handed strike, its duration and volume, the type of drum, and which part of the drum receives the hit.

( )

Deborah Wong writes that *don is a sound of power, or a powerful sound, or a signal that power is present*. Don arrives with a deep, rich timbre. *The sound of don assigns the feeling of power to things and people. Don is Japanese but moves around the world with/*

in taiko. Don: the strike of bachi on a drumhead, deep and resonant. Don: a single, forceful movement, originated by the lower body. Don: a fist meeting a wall. Don: the skull meeting a migraine. Don: a slap behind a closed door. Don: waves slamming a shore.

( )

On December 8, 1941, the Japanese army attacked Hong Kong, where British and Canadian soldiers were stationed. The Battle of Hong Kong (also known as the Fall) followed the Japanese navy's attack on Pearl Harbor. During WWII, the US and Canada incarcerated nearly 150,000 Japanese people in prison camps. Vancouver MP Ian MacKenzie saw the war as an opportunity to control the Japanese *from the Rockies to the sea*. He said, *I do not believe the Japanese are an assimilable race.*

( )

North American kumi-daiko players share a common mythology. After incarceration, Nikkei communities used drumming as a tactic of cultural memory, following in the lineage of three primary groups: San Francisco Taiko, Kinnara Taiko, or San Jose Taiko. These groups are taxonomized as a shorthand for professionalism, spirituality, and social justice, respectively. Taiko as an instrument is much older, with roots in religious ritual and military theatre. In feudal Japan, taiko were used to marshal troops, call out orders, or set a marching pace: six paces to each beat of the drum.

( )

The Japanese army's covert Unit 731 experimented on Chinese and Korean prisoners—children, communists, farmers—*logs*, according to their torturers. Between 1936 and 1945, roughly fourteen thousand people were murdered. Deliberate infection by syphilis, typhus, cholera; forced frostbite; vivisection without anaesthesia. *What's really scary is, I don't have any nightmares of what I've done*, said Ken Yuasa, a Japanese army doctor. Unit 731 was officially known as the Epidemic Prevention and Water Purification Department of the Kwantung Army. Warfare can be called science if the data collected serves war's purpose. Evidence can be killed if there are no documented survivors. Some violence is meaningless. A sentence can also use circular logic to distance itself from meaning. This paragraph is full of meaningless sentences.

( )

In an introduction to his own poem, "we are rejoicing as japanese america is falling into dust," shō yamagushiku writes: *A particularly disorienting fact: recovery / healing work after "nikkei wartime incarceration" repeatedly becomes the work of reviving the somatics of Japanese imperialism.*

( )

I started learning taiko because I put too much stock in semantics. In taiko, blank space is dynamic, filled with breath and movement. I wanted to shout syllables that could mean many things, including holding or denoting silence: *su*, *ha*, *i-ya*, *so-re*. I wanted to let my voice crack. Often, when triggered or in crisis, I go non-verbal. My care team has developed an emoji code for such moments, when I can't communicate my needs in words. Hedgehog: phone call while I fall asleep. Robot: quiet and companionable walk. Rice: warm meal or groceries, delivered to my door.

( )

Years before I picked up my first bachi, I watched a YouTube video of the taiko group I later joined. One of the comments read, This band can topple a government. Another: To hear these battle cries would intimidate any coming army. Drum on Lady Warriors!

( )

Wong writes of taiko not as an object of sound, or even of the body, but *as body*. An iterative exchange between music and physicality. Movement generates sound, sound produces a reason for movement. The body is an instrument whose purpose is practice, not legibility. When enough people are chanting, the words dissolve into pure resonance. Noise fills up a room without invitation. Noise is intrusive, intimate—what resists absorption into a narrative structure.

( )

To house the drums, we rent a studio. To pay our rent, we rely on gigs, grants accorded by state-funded infrastructures. To book gigs, we peddle our sound to supermarket openings, school assemblies, weddings, park concerts, union conventions, academic conferences, restaurant openings, business meetings, award ceremonies, marches, rallies, community festivals, non-profit celebration dinners. Alienated from lineage, optimized for profit. In the slippage between language and rhythm, I don the branded T-shirt. I smile for the crowd.

( )

My first and third uncles on my mom's side died during Japan's occupation of Hong Kong, in the midst of the Second World War. The occupation is sometimes called 三年零八個月. Three years and eight months, metonymic for the timespan of terror, hunger, and violence under Japanese imperial administration. Between December 25, 1941 and August 15, 1945, an estimated ten thousand people were executed. Many more were tortured and raped.

( )

What sounds are soldiers? Whose bodies are instruments? Choreographed gestures echo down a line of drummers. Sound is a consequence of silence. Care is a touch that travels through time. The core keeps balance. The kiai keeps time. Vibration tones the vagus nerve which, in turn, signals safety to our bodies—regardless of whether or not real safety is there.

( )

When I say doctor, I don't mean only doctors, I mean anyone with the power to force a cure, and failing cure, a cage. When I say don, I mean: a communism of action, not ideas. What gathers me, in the wild beyond when language fails? A simple syllable or two would suffice. Do you want company? Who should I call if you get arrested? Can I come hold your hand? Hedgehog. Robot. Rice.

( )

Jane Shi remixes the Chinese characters for self, love, and mouth into a new word for autism, meaning: *those who allow themselves to love themselves. This new word,* Shi writes, *reminded me that we do not have to tell each other we love each other to express love. It reminded me that speaking is not the only way to communicate.* History speaks too, in run-on silences. In practice, I love to improvise. Making sound with others, again and again. Meaning is what, on a good day, I allow myself to fail at producing. What might, without attunement, be understood as noise—irksome, unmusical. Inside: a tumble of colours, sensations, and impulses. Outside: two fingers tapping the table, a hum, a sigh, a blink, a rock. *Drum on!* Sometimes, I'm not trying to communicate. I want to be felt.

VISUAL SCORE (CHRONIC ILLNESS)

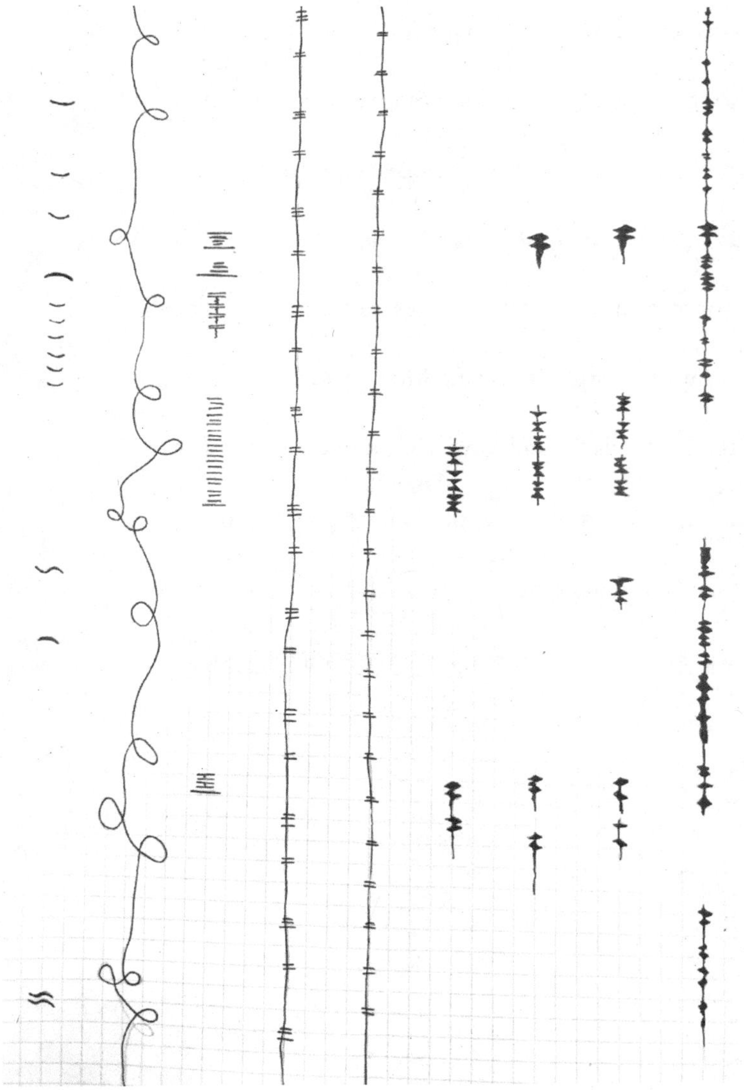

[performance score:

this score can be read in any direction, by any instrument

for example: three rocks, a Singer, and a loop station

or: heat pad, melodica, cyclobenzaprine, naproxen

if a patient record is printed, where does notation fail

not to overidentify with a prescription or a diagnosis

symptoms organize sound into a grid of checkboxes

the beat falls behind; time clinging to a warped mark

the future is a promise, please rate from 1–10

pain is a spinal sentence, a long hallway, flute: I

wet and hollow centre, with no meaning or metre]

AGAINST NOSTALGIA

like my mother, love was once magnetic.
dressed in an old lace curtain, her sweet
potato face. I fell for love like a stone

into a well of memory. lily bulbs and pickled
mustard root, eaten at the hospital. stones
sunk ruthlessly into organs. eight siblings

sharing a single sweet potato, the reek
of an army outside the door. the eldest brother
donning his dead face, pickled in the red

light of war. blood, or the juice
from a can of American tomatoes.
under the sterile gown my mother

donned her prettiest lace. memory
curtains my face. love's tongue, toothless
as a hospital, a well, barren of mothers

of tongues trained in the language of lilies.
how often in an evening love says my name.
meanwhile I bleed onto the lace. meat

sweating on the plate. no rice to eat, but ground
melons for cheap, inked red as they were
with memory. I ask love how to sever

past from present. the hospital beckons me
home. history swells between the curtains.

DIALECTICAL BEHAVIOUR THERAPY

the air on the other side of the door
does not belong to us. you record

your shadow on my threshold, downstroke
of intimacy, a moment full of keys. words

double repeatedly until they lose all meaning:
community, healing, family. suspended nostalgia

deters linearity. what was grammar? what is
insanity? perhaps a group chat, a sleepover. I

drop my senses on the floor when you reach
for me. the syntax not of camaraderie

but recurrence. every kiss is perfectly round
like a dream. does language overdetermine?

my mind wrinkles like a peach pit, late summer.
illicit and sweet, I jar its secret at the sink. desire

disorients. I don't want to understand it. between us, life
drips. then hardens. at the protest, three officers draw

fingers from belt loops to riot grips. a movement
equidistant between music and silence. threat of rubber

bullets, pens set to ticket. sometimes loyalty leads
to self-destruction. the question isn't who has endured

but who hasn't. a year or a sentence, whatever ends
first. our continuation is a disclosure by degrees. cadre

of mountain marigold disturbing the drab terrace
where tear gas disperses. I capture that night

with my drugstore camera. water bottles outside
the jail, cold pizza, escape of sound and tenderness.

AGAINST EULOGY

one month since touch, he looms loud
in my mind. Li Wenliang, first

to warn of fear and masks. one
month from then, he was dead, versed

in the slant truths of a state.
what lies in a month? trees burst

bare to bloom while I sleep. what
do I know of bone? of thirst?

spring brims with the wrong heat. death
slips from hand to hand like mail.

in Hong Kong, bars close two weeks
on pain of six months in jail.

Wuhan lines up to burn loved ones.
ash clouds the eyes, sore and pale.

with no right to mourn, a girl
dives ten floors down. the moon wails.

time dusts the yard in green. one
tenth through the break, and whose cheap

deaths will get us there? the route
to you spans ten more months, steep

price for shared breath. I lift words
all May, I verse your way, heap

clean books on your porch. on my
own I come, then cry, then sleep.

so many words we know for touch:
to press or tap, nudge or poke

to prod, to push, to pat, to
glance. a smudge of heat, a stroke.

weight on my chest, my palm on
my cheek. my guard breaks like yolk

on bread. I long, I rage, I
speak, I crack my hands with soap.

the dead in Wuhan do not speak,
bleached of noise and heat, the signs

of life they hold, those who live
and live and do not cry, lined

up though they are to choose grave
sites. a grey weight tilts each spine.

守得雲開見月明.
grey clouds drink the moon's dead shine.

two months slide by like thin paint.
I strain from bed to desk, climb

hour by hour out of dread. what
comes first, the hope or pain? mime

of thirst or mime of rain? my
wrists bend the clock for crip time,

drip time, slow sand time, grief time
with no end, no cure or rhyme.

yes, my mind drops Wuhan when
our own late fire strikes. from first

known case to last, four months pass.
the state says not to tell. versed

in the words of risk, they stay.
low risk, high, lies fit to burst.

am I the West? I, who dons
masks, burns rice, chews stones for thirst?

from bed, I watch an ant, dust-
caught, toil to get free. we faced

these months with words of war, and
now this lull, this drought of touch.

close the shops. stop work, drop debts.
I have no more tricks for pain.

each new day tastes of raw meat.
I am in the mood for rain.

MOVEMENT II

[audio score:

another slow march of objects and edges:
knife in jar, chain on drum, organ under
the space between word and image. then
a dissonance knotted to meaning as guess
as association to a sound. a kind of gravity
or reason. how it clings, film-like, to real
things, experiences, echoes, a reel of images

rising:
          red stone in the wet dirt
                    damp stains on one side of the deathbed

disorganized violence does not exist, the question is scale:

at Blida-Joinville, Fanon treats both French and Algerian patients,
soldiers, fedayeen, from 1953 to 1956

sunlight crosses the clinic over the course of a day
                    psychiatrists clink at the cocktail party

madness resists mastery yet, to attenuate the violence
of a colonial system: an impossibility, as revealed
          in Fanon's resignation letter:

I cannot continue to bear a responsibility
at no matter what cost, on the false pretext that
                              there is nothing else to be done

there is something else to be done]

SONOGRAM

sound, short bursts

by dolphin, cannon, most species of bat

a consequence of echolocation

to situate the self according to distant,
invisible objects

prey, or mother, or monarch, for instance

a string plucked by history's hand, ringing

mother, appended to lode or land or tongue
denotes an origin

a way of being, filled with conquest

notes follow a time signature, a treble clef

lyric: a wet rock, shivering in the sun

note: a sound compressed into pitch and duration

to strike the eye, the ear, a breakable
radius

notation, chords positioned inside a regulatory structure

echolocation, to calculate a separation based on volume and time

the shadow of which may remain undetected

the shattering of which may remain undocumented

There are two ways of rejecting the revolution. The first is to refuse to see it where it exists; the second is to see it where it manifestly will not occur.

FÉLIX GUATTARI, *CHAOSOPHY*

There should be no therapeutic act that has not been previously established as a revolutionary act.

DR. WOLFGANG HUBER

TURN ILLNESS INTO A WEAPON

Sozialistisches Patientenkollektiv (SPK), Heidelberg

The psychiatrist Wolfgang Huber founded the SPK in 1970 at the Heidelberg University polyclinic, based on the ethos:

> Illness is a contradiction created by capitalism.
> A protest driving the system to its own destruction.
> A patient is part of a revolutionary class.

Prominent figures in the field of anti-psychiatry distanced themselves.

A patient buries a pain scale in a field.

A student acclimatizes to therapy and test papers.

A field is a paltry substitute for hydrocodone, ibuprofen,
naproxen, tramadol.

Pain transcends rhetoric.

Rhetoric transforms pain.

Patients formed committees to run their own clinics. Free spaces
for political therapy.

Patients publishing demands in university magazines were put
on higher doses of medication.

The *kidney-stone* is the same as the stone cast into the
commanding centre of capitalism.

A control room is a field of machinery.

The university clinic fired Huber, his enemies armed with anti-Hegelian rhetoric, prisons, and police.

Police who beat patients protesting on the university
administrator's posh, parochial lawn.

In the 1890s, Kraepelin—considered the grandfather of the Diagnostic and Statistical Manual of Mental Disorders (DSM)—directed Heidelberg's department of psychiatry.

The university under Kraepelin and then the Nazis stamped patients for euthanasia according to diagnosis, class, their capacity to be cured.

The psychiatrist prescribes me Prozac, even though I try to convince her I'm not depressed.

Without insurance, the pills cost $50 a month.

Professional care produces the idea of property.

A patient produces a therapeutic praxis.

Contradictory and social; surplus and singular.

Pill bottles accumulate in my bedside drawer.

The federal disability benefit pays up to $200 a month.

The German Criminal Code (section 129) justified warrantless searches and arrests, dissidents detained.

Alleged SPK members were held in physical and acoustic isolation, in a white cell with fluorescent lighting on for twenty-four hours per day, for several months.

Sometimes healing requires violence.

Sometimes healing requires occupying the administrator's office.

Holding history in one fist, a hand grenade in the other.

SYNTAX LESSONS

Match infinitives on the left with prepositions on the right.

to lock down one's arms

to glue oneself to the asphalt

to declare a picket line

to orchestrate the prison break

to describe the living of my beloveds (aracelis girmay)

to forfeit the liberal fantasy

to defend one's homeland at gunpoint

to be one among many

to mend the language of dissent

across a highway bridge

in the colonial parade

on the arms factory green

in the mall atrium's metal eye

at the courthouse facing criminal trial

of diversity statements and parliamentary seats

over pipeline sites the rivers running underneath

masked, targeted, unrelenting

before the enemy poets void language of all meaning

MADNESS BELONGS TO THE PEOPLE

Bethel House, Urakawa

In the opening scene of Karen Nakamura's YouTube documentary
Bethel: Community and Schizophrenia in Northern Japan

house members improvise a tune
about schizophrenia and papayas.

Everything goes into the lyrics:
insomnia, fences, cutting, snow.

Feet and hands stomp out the beat.

Isn't schizophrenia terrible? (PAPAYA)

Isn't mental illness wonderful? (PAPAYA)

Growing up, I was convinced there was no such thing
as a friend who wouldn't leave me.

The adults who raised me convinced me.

Memory lodges in the body and becomes personality.

If I forced myself onto the front of my patients' stage,
the psychiatrist says, *that would be bad theatre.*

*Who wants to watch a movie where the psychiatrist
makes himself the centre?*

The ocean sits off-screen, quiet and calm.

A lid twisted onto the jar of the mind.

If I had to describe what was happening in my head, I would point to the tuning fork trembling.

Friction with the air produces a sound.

Friction with time produces understanding.

I want to take care of the parts of myself I can't change.

Annually, Bethel mounts a contest for Hallucinations and Delusions.

One man is extremely anxious, convinced a UFO has come to abduct him. The spaceship is a two-seater. He has to choose another person to go with him. The house members convince him that he needs a UFO license to ride in the spaceship; a license which he can only obtain at the space centre.

Who thinks he should go to the space centre? one member asks. In other words, the psychiatrist's office.

Unanimously, everyone raises their hands;
he goes;
everyone wins.

Some members work at a seaweed packing factory during the day. Fingers dance with plastic bags; mouths with gossip.

Don't move your hands, move your lips is the work slogan.

At their weekly social skills training, members role-play different approaches to real life situations.

After each round, they talk about what was good
what could be improved.

To test the utility of a collective response.

To practice directly expressing a feeling.

A woman storms out of a group meeting in tears. Other members have told her she leads a degenerate life because she doesn't have a boyfriend, and she smells bad. *Even if it's true you shouldn't say it to her face,* someone says. Still others step in, *Let's stop this,* they say, *and work together.*

A staff member distributes cookies shaped like ducks.

Reducing the dosage of medication allows the problems to surface, and the healing to begin.

Collecting friends is more stable than curing.

As long as we're sick, we will have each other.

Madness as a conductor with sticky hands, clapping

to keep time.

Curtains of snow disguise the sounds of a carol.

The members, out of view, sing in Japanese. I take a moment to recognize the tune.

Silent Night, Kiyoshi kono yoru.

As the credits fade, the members are singing still.

We're all first-class sickos!

It's okay to be alive.

SONOGRAM (UNIT 731)

the air in this house is winter, always, and full of music

they constructed the clinic around a central prison

social practice, seaweed packages, therapy three times a week

experiments reserved for the healthiest subjects

you overwater the sansevieria; mould silvers
beneath the starter leaves

sometimes care is an encounter of control

in the kitchen, your lover arches her back before the stove

cyanide, chloroform; what the doctors considered play

earlier, she sharpened a blade on a soaked stone

the doctors called them log; specimen; hardly a face

madness becomes a fish, slippery in the hands

pathogens deployed in fleas, wells, in snacks
distributed to locals

you have everything you ever wanted

without light, blood running red is a matter of faith

MADNESS IS A STRATEGY

Before madness meant rage, it meant insanity. Gemædde: to be out of one's mind. Sharing a linguistic root with the Latin verb mutare: to change, to go, to move.

Anger derives from Old Norse angr, or: grief, sorrow, distress, affliction. My life grew around what, within me, needed protection. Later, my life's vocabulary—to wing, to wild—grew incongruent with the script of normalcy—to work the clock, to write the cheques, post-dated, for rent.

Madness disturbs the book. Anger bubbles the page, blooms a gathering. A red breach. I tend to boil over. The place my madness knows as home: a low-pressure front, a reservoir of panic. A muscular humidity, threatening heat.

To the state, mass murder is a matter of economy. Years into a pandemic, masking becomes an uncommon accommodation. Words interrupt, but they cannot solve. Nor anger alone, translated into bodies in the street. A call-and-response of strategy and pragmatism is not sufficient. Language cannot replace movement, only approximate it.

I learned about anger in my father's house. Belts unlooped, blurred doorways in my dreams. He raised us to be obedient, not happy. I couldn't tell the difference. Doubt condenses into a myth about the self. Only time revised my understanding. Thermal shadow of a mother long dead. Her wayward frequencies.

Preverbal, as in: before language or memory. A contraction in the eyes. A hardening of the chest.

The symptoms titled madness are so often strategies for survival. Our bodies clarify our ancestors' lifetimes. Pour water into an empty container; theory fills every space.

My instinct is to nod, make small, tame breath. To scream on the inside only, wield a smile, optimize for labour, to leave the frame. In Chinese, the characters for happiness depict an open heart; sadness, a heart that's hurt. Energy, or passion: a hot heart, a heart on fire.

Many lineages connect power to one's core. Martial arts and qigong, taiko drumming. Silence spills with movement. Breath tells a story of what matters. What loosens it; what grinds it down. Madness is my structure of possibility. I don't mean this as a metaphor. I trust the people who have sat with me there, outside the world. Every day, I've handed them my life.

In madness, I am more porous—the task is to need others without consuming them. Sentences collapse into sound. Sound glows without meaning. My mind lights up, no longer self-contained. The world transpires, then continues to transpire. The doctors give up their jobs so they can take care of the people. The state administers language, but it doesn't know how to dance.

To build bonds that outlast periods of crisis, political parties, the constrictions of work and rent. *Certain modes of relating can crack us open*, write Clémence x. Clémentine. *We are learning how to unleash our desires to the point that they rupture with capital.*

Madness cutting the noise, unwinding a signal for elsewhere.

If a riot is a feeling and a sound. I offer my language to my madness. My madness takes whatever it wants. My mouth, my memory, my movement, my breath. My body finds freedom in the places where semantics fall short. Squares the chest, stacks the shoulders. Arms linked against an oncoming police line. Vertebra by vertebra, bearing up, unfurling my spine into the sky.

A sound can become a feeling of power. Silence, the space for my breath to synchronize with yours. Madness is not contagious. When the music plays, my body moves of its own accord.

To live beside madness has required me to follow my body through my own cruelties. The silences I wielded at myself, my ex-lover. The knife I dragged through suicidal hours. A dissonance not forgotten, but knotted around me like a scarf. I am necessary, I am not special. Can I imagine growing old? Can I imagine being satisfied by my own life?

CENTRE

may you enter with care
wherever your breath lands
may you not bear this tenderness alone
whenever the light catches in you
may the future bend down to hold you
as the waters draw forth your dead
like bruises, your newborn light
your shadow, huddled by the window
may you meet the ocean with memory
may language move you to action
may all the locked doors sing inside you

may all the locked doors sing inside you
may language move you to action
may you meet the ocean with memory
your shadow, huddled by the window
like bruises, your newborn light
as the waters draw forth your dead
may the future bend down to hold you
whenever the light catches in you
may you not bear this tenderness alone
wherever your breath lands
may you enter with care

[visual description:

two circles formed of text and broken
at each end, death turns the self inside
out, a hole for the body to pass through

may you enter with care
wherever your breath lands
may you not bear this tenderness alone
whenever the light catches in you
may the future bend down to hold you
as the waters draw forth your dead
like bruises, your newborn light
your shadow, huddled by the window
may you meet the ocean with memory
may language move you to action
may all the locked doors sing inside you

may all the locked doors sing inside you
may language move you to action
may you meet the ocean with memory
your shadow, huddled by the window
like bruises, your newborn light
as the waters draw forth your dead
may the future bend down to hold you
whenever the light catches in you
may you not bear this tenderness alone
wherever your breath lands
may you enter with care]

MOVEMENT III

[audio score:

snare and tom and sometimes every day is too dense to think let
alone practice. the task of copper pipes and cymbals stretching
sound over a frame, or Franco Basaglia's relation to psychiatry,
more theoretical than clinical. anti-fascist memories of prison,
to Trieste in 1971 where he directed asylum activities, papers
co-written with Franca Ongaro. still now, the drum vibrates, still
bells and plates,

any silence

a measurement of the space between self and other. *when we*
say no to the asylum, we say no to the misery of the world, Basaglia
wrote, and would not abandon the SPK. the distance between
madness and prophecy

is a property of time. to close down

the hospital, host militant conferences theatrical projects free
housing on the former grounds. as

close to revolution, yet excess

slogans (external) do not treat real suffering (internal), now what]

ECHOLOCATION

I join a somatic practice group online in September 2020. In our disjointed rooms, we gather candles, blankets, vessels of chamomile. On screen, our worlds touch at the edges. We stare at ourselves as others speak, until our own faces go alien, words repeated until they relinquish all meaning. Someone forgets to unmute. Their lips move without a sound. Someone else activates their microphone as children and dogs turn siren in the background.

( )

Years after lockdown, COVID-19 persists. My friends take me raving. Four on the floor, masks in our pockets, 120 beats per minute. Technology automates the distortion of signals. Synth driving a dissociated pleasure. In the absence of light, I learn my lover by their movements. *Practice* names the pleasure of repetition. Listening is a form of touch. Silence closes its mouth around desire. Scrap of synchrony, pulse of togetherness. To turn sound into a weapon. To participate in life when the state wants us dead.

( )

Techno and house are Black fugitive forms, derived from post-industrial scenes in Detroit and other cities. An alchemical tactic, to transform the machinery of one's containment into a sonics of freedom and release. In the '60s and '70s, doctors diagnosed Black civil rights activists with schizophrenia, or protest psychosis. What sound they could not control; what desires they tried to contain. Information exchanged via aural artifact. Worlds encoded as noise, the landscape sequenced into beat. In his introduction to Stefano Harney and Fred Moten's *The*

Undercommons, Jack Halberstam writes: *Listening to cacophony and noise tells us that there is a wild beyond to the structures we inhabit and that inhabit us*. A rave is not a call to order. I only know dances with no choreography. *The path to the wild beyond is paved with refusal*. Freedom is a demand, not a broadcast subject to rules and regulations.

( )

I hold tension in my jaw and forehead, where a dolphin catches echoes. I'm predisposed to chronic pain and opposed to classical romance. The doctor says temporomandibular joint disorder. The therapist says intergenerational trauma. The dentist says $400 mouthguard. Health insurance requires normative labour or a state-sanctioned intimacy. A ticket to dance costs $20. And yet pleasure can serve more sedative purposes. I move into a neighbourhood with Pilates studios on every corner. Alienated workers numb their discontent with repetitive core movements. A regime requires volunteers. The psychiatrist's prescription does not preclude the possibility of uprising, nor does it call uprising's name.

( )

What if school, as we used it on a daily basis, signalled not the name of a process or institution through which we could be indoctrinated, asks Alexis Pauline Gumbs. When disease decimated dolphin populations in the Mediterranean Sea, they located each other through kinship echo—new practices of school by which they could survive. *What if school was the scale at which we could care for each other and move together. I am wondering if we could trade the image of "family" for the practice of school.*

( )

In a speech given to garner support for the Black Panther Party when Huey P. Newton was in jail, Fred Hampton said: *If you don't have any practice, then you can't walk across the street and chew gum at the same time.* Our somatic group facilitator introduces a practice for ancestor work. To choose an ancestor, and repeat their words out loud, to map the contours of their sound. I speak their names with my hands, my feet: Grace Lee Boggs, Stacey Park Milbern, June Jordan, Yuri Kochiyama.

( )

For a season, I live a fifteen-minute walk from the Kobechenonk; a river that goes by this name, and many others. I gather myself on a bench, to practice listening. The farthest vibrations: wheels on gravel, the bell of children laughing. Then the closest: my breath, my blood, the friction of skin against fabric. In between: the leaves, the wind, the river folding in on itself. Far from family, I learn the world by its distance. *Beauty is something opening,* the poet Bahar Orang writes, *and if you are lucky, the thing opening is you, your body, your palms and your feet, so you are more surface to press against the earth.*

( )

All senses are tactile: the places where I brushes up against the skin of the world. Cones and rods respond to light, an ear thrums against the brain, blueberry bursting on the tongue. Hampton's point: *Power anywhere where there's people. Power anywhere where there's people.* Music holds history. No image is neutral. To echolocate is to flirt with vibration, to receive what survives the distance and returns. On the dance floor, skin to sound, devastating to admit it—I did not feel alone. Self is the echo that togetherness makes. This page, in your hands, holds merely words. Memories of touch.

MOVEMENT NOTATION

[performance score:

read volume, direction, intonation from the line

turn time into touch in the international arrivals terminal

waiting is a pulse, clipped gait, circling the metronome

someone you knew is in love with you in another country

the distance is not a metaphor, but a silence that leaks

you lack: a theory of change, in relation and in movement

you state your devotion into the security camera

if the officer denies you, request a written record

of your path, a dissident mark slashed from negative space

abandon any bureaucratic enclosure, any implied metre

the chorus repeats until your body is emptied of sound]

ECHO SYSTEM

I don't call myself a musician until I am tasked to compose. Five years drumming yet the drums remain a wildness.

Routed through music, I relinquish my allegiance to meaning.

Notes spilling over a time signature, a staff. A system of predefined syllables.

girmay says: *Please don't forget to let your language rest, to make things without words.*

And still, words seep into the frame. To say: play this drum, or that one. To count time. To inscribe blank space with motion then enact with another body my devised choreography.

Notation presents a problem of translation. How to record one's breath and silence and forms of struggle? How to locate the pulse that animates such movement?

Composition: brushstrokes, one after another, articulate a landscape, a river in motion, a single character, profligate with meaning.

Chinese calligraphy, like drumming, is an art of negative space. If the artist rushes, the character compresses, limbs run together. With hesitation, the ink wavers, leaking through the page. Your problems with writing, my teacher says, are your problems with living. My own characters emerge unbalanced, off-kilter.

Five slashes conjure stones, a riverbank. Over time, five tapers etymologically to four, before finally becoming legible as a single idea: water.

In composition, I pursue odd time signatures. Threes, fives, sevens. Steeped in duples, the draw of even numbers, my untrained ear registers these at first as lurching, irregular. To play with precision, I must internalize a constant, droning count, the space between body and mind a flood of numbers.

Flood: one of my first cellular memories, an egg in an egg inside my grandmother. A slim probability, not yet realized. Loss in our blood, a day the colour of mud. Her parents, her familiar landscapes, the village of her childhood home, carried in the river's wake.

I've always feared the ocean, even when I became enraptured with the mythology of mermaids. Half-human, half-fish, I dreamed of living inside of what killed my family. The sound of light on my scales, my breath bending water, its harbour extending endlessly before me.

My grandmother survived, hidden in the folds of circumstance. Two teachers adopted her, and the boy who would become my grandfather. I can't ask her whether she would describe herself as lucky.

My mother died alone in the hospital, decades later, an unexpected flooding in the lungs and kidneys. In her lungs and kidneys; complications from childbirth. Even now, my diction accrues an illusion of distance. The child was me. My birth, breaching her body.

The drums do not offer an easily parsable melody. Their sound sits somewhere between noise and music: resistant to semantics, blurry at the edges.

In my mother's aftermath, the silence was never silent, but filled with other people's reactions, a rupture through which I poured my own disjointed conditionals.

If the drum could be home. If reversal were a possibility. If my ache could speak. If movement holds memory. If, in another timeline, the river does not touch our family. If my life cost nothing. If I were a body of water. If I were not. If I were not. If I were not. If I were not. If I were not.

I ask my fellow drummers, then: to tear the margin between poet and performer, to write the chorus collectively. When I press our creations together at the seams, a thing like a fish's tail emerges. Sonic, wet and shimmering.

When it comes to home, we are always leaving and returning, compelled by the drum's gravity. This, in the end, is what I know best: recuperating song from echo, pulse from fragment, a sequence of gestures, a river's polyphony.

[performance score:

1 = tenses collapse, a bankless river

2 = crumpled fabric, crowds accustomed to a police barricade

3 = tear gas diverted from open eyes, any ruptured membrane

4 = in the folds of the mind, faces leak into the foreground

5 = stacking stones, a promise only struggle can make]

IF I WERE A BODY OF WATER

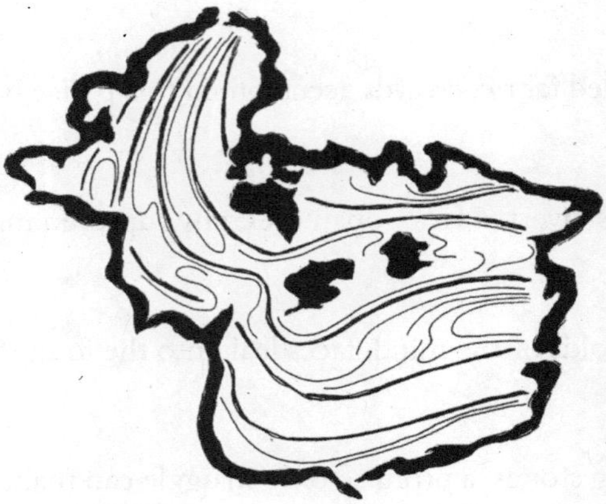

to imagine the world as mapped by a fish

longitude composed of a lingering lack, a sentence
spanning decades

sonic input of burnt rice and shrapnel, what once was

childhood; now is nothing but memory and breath

a homeland brushed with barbed wire and tear gas

having mostly rehearsed the cadence of hospitals
and serrated edges

that labour can steal from our bodies even the water

in a lifetime, how arrival loses ground to departure

I sharpen my ink against displacement, wherever it occurs

and so attempt to listen to the dead, their illegible movements

grief traces the lungs, pierces night's folded corners

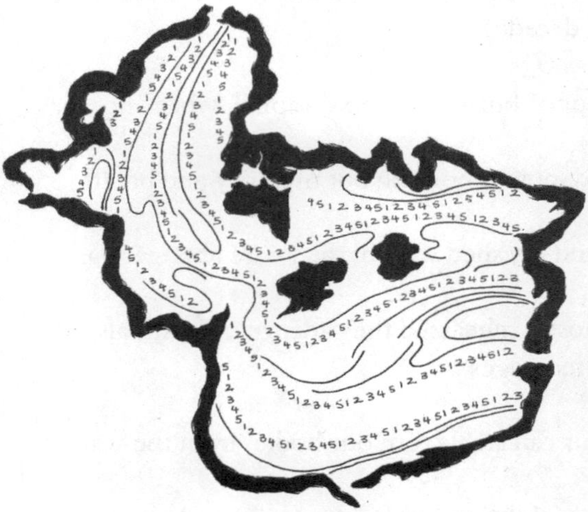

[performance score:

1 = distance dismantles sound, faith dimmed by
a loss of frequency

2 = when the hourglass brims, drag your tail over
a surface of water

3 = to resist is to return, to dream is to reach

4 = each inhale, a sleepless yesterday
each exhale, a crumbling empire

5 = where tide ends and movement begins
take measure of the ocean's form, limb by limb]

TUNING FORK

in the space between
anything and ancestor

let us attune to the frequency
of what has not yet been lost

two daughters wed beneath a birch tree
twelve lilies, pink, wrapped in paper

inside the sound of sunset is a red banner
proclaiming NO MORE RENTS

no more trains on their way to lengthen pipelines
no defendants arrested against the tracks
no bicycles painted white at the intersection

may these days of ending allow us still
to water the marigold seedlings, morning-bright

let there be fig squares, broken in half
let there be music and synchronized movement

let there be the goodbyes we waited for
our whole lives, let there be our whole lives

our laughter, effervescing and errant

I would choose it
again, yes, every time

FREE THE PEOPLE FREE THE LAND

in the register of elsewhere, our screens
elide empire's strategies—lies sutured clean

to silence. a mythology of innocence. what
ellipsis could satisfy the dead? only say

every word we must, only—can language exceed
neon vests on horses, a hospital spilled

across grey rubble. when the day breaks,
it shatters. blood in the dust, mud in the rafters.

what home was but a life, four walls, transferred
to memory. no, love cannot be merely theory.
beneath the expressway, cardboard bellows

and the concrete ends in cold water. to the building
scaffold floating flags of survival, we owe more

than the anaesthetics of story. to turn our arms
toward the chain-link fence. to tear it to the ground.
to hear the land, how it dreams again of touch.

what we call revolution attunes itself to care
when we say we are all we have—we have
never been without power or each other. if now

the scaffold cracks—even for a moment—I am
flying, my tongue wet, my mouth full of seeds.

MOVEMENT IV

[audio score:

it has begun—has it begun? it being
what we are listening to, which moves
and is moved against metre, or tone
given its tendency to bell, its bass undertow the sound of
unidentifiable switches flipped in a row or bow on cardboard
producing a moan or sand against washing
board, ratchet, balloon singing on skin I am beholden
not to know too much not to answer the diagnostic
questions when asked for beauty, sudden and unexpected when
it arrives in organ harmonies, knee-deep
                                        in my mind its diametrics—

to open the doors
of the asylum (Berrechid)

to patrol the perimeter
of the mind (Dr. Ziou Ziou)

synecdoche for madness
in the collective imaginary

sanctuary of freedom, short-
lived, no less worthwhile

chairs spread in an oval
pattern in the garden

invitations arranged to local
press, townspeople, artists

poetry is a way of organizing attunement
silence is a way of organizing presence

each mural producing an us
for ninety seconds of looking

desire was the wildness
we couldn't name

memory is a room inside
me with tilted floors
each cure is collective

the sonic weight of a
collapsing square
each suffering is singular]

SONOGRAM

acidic the kick of drums in an emptied room
in other words, the self has never been enough

that din of image, affect, sensation, pouring through

echo of I-lessness, thrum of touch

in the tumult of protest, I felt what couldn't be heard

madness, the ancestral choir

madness, communal furor, strikes me out of my skin

I inhabit the breach between language and music

drawn to whatever beating crowd, whatever fleeting plural

what gravity, to make our dreams percussive

to crescendo the body against the mind's door

TERMINUS

half human, half fish. mutiny
folded when squeezed in a fist.

the difference between rebel
and monster depends on who

drafts the myth. 水上人, the people
on the water. deviant, ancestor,

militant, general. a rebellion, once
fractured, turned feral. in 1997

Hong Kong changes hands
to the Chinese from the British.

decades later, in heat-proof gloves, protesters
neutralize tear gas canisters with water

bottles. these days, I trust nothing
as much as I trust my anger.

settler hands conjure a wall, settler poison
marks the water, without which no one

will live. at an ultrasound appointment—who
turns the transducer? who winds

the key?—images induced on a screen
indicate proof of a future. we exist

there. do we exist there? do we
                    exist? there, beyond
            memorial, beyond military law—

the museum hunts what cannot be found.
each echo outlives the original sound.

When the Algerians reject any method which does not include violence . . . they know that such madness alone can deliver them from colonial repression.

FRANTZ FANON, *THE WRETCHED OF THE EARTH*

MADNESS BELONGS TO THE PEOPLE

before the Algerians revolted, Fanon treated
French soldiers charged with torture

electroshock, insulin coma. discredited
cures tick by, unnumbered
a myth travels
dog-eared, from then to here

in somatic therapy training, you watch
videos of veterans punching pillows, secured
in the hands of white women

you quit your private practice,
divest from regulatory certifications

the DSM fails to identify
an original cause

disturbed by the idea that nation-states
could exhibit trauma responses—

yet the grid of blamelessness
excludes your face

a family is a funeral
at distances you can't afford to pay

with every encounter, the mind
dissolves your personality, then
reconstitutes it

madness as form response. madness as
plucked string. madness as the lover's
first impression: perfectly round, impossible

to recover. *Madness*, Fanon wrote
in his dissertation, *is*
a pathology of freedom

inside your mind, rocks soar over fences

inside the glass office, you shred the papers
on which peace was promised

if colonizers call revolutionary consciousness

"collective psychosis"
if desire merits batons and water cannons

who will diagnose the system, since there is no outside—

the hospital machines' beeping
the psychiatrist's screening
blurs the self into a blood-wet noise

ECHO CHAMBER

Before my breath was mine, it was my mother's. Her echo
and pulse. Her misfired intentions, her shrink-wrapped
future.

Unplugging the white noise machine, static cuts
to silence. As a therapist, I tended to porousness.
I couldn't help but approach in the first person.
I, we, those brief wicks of intimacy. Burned out.

Forests flame in Quebec and here, the skies stained all
summer. Drone of smog, fists of charred blue.

Wildfire smoke and COVID-19 target the respiratory cilia.
Tiny lung hairs mobilize, an essential hum, waving mucus
upward to the throat. If the cilia get damaged, mucus
collects, lungs clench. Eventually they drown in their own
fluid.

Humidity erodes a sense of self. Skin dissolved into heat.
Dulcet din of splash pads and swimming pools in public
parks. Shelters packed to spill. Condos, cool and empty,
above our heads. By 2050, heat waves will occur five times
more often. Sweat blurs the day's edges.

Two screens, in the mind's theatre. Two clotted streams of imagery. Drought, blaze, storm, deluge. Their potentials, their destructions, diametric.

Then again, grief and anger are not binaries. Their meanings are not fixed. Neither are excess and lack, nor the colours of objects, the skies today burning red, orange, yellow, even green.

Mucus, trapping bacteria and virus, then expelled, iridescent in the sink. Thick fluid which, when amassed in the lungs, causes inflammation. Hushes the breath. Danger and defence, a continuous loop.

All night, I wheeze into the silence. The hours, a bowl of congealed blue. Absence of witness, of a solicitous mother dotting VapoRub on my throat. She, too, knew asthma. Solitary wakefulness. The underside of illness. Similarities I speak out loud and document, seeking an etiological connection.

Each utterance an island, a node of want.

What is the dew point at which dreams dampen? Every organizer faces the accusations—idealism, naivete, get out of your echo chamber. Sooner or later, the thumb of cynicism begins to press on belief. Loss accrues a percussive force.

A dream: to recuperate a historical lack. To record an echo, to write its wayward passage through the museum's galleries. The curator stitches a narrative from scraps of myth. The medic presses gauze
into a wound.

Preparing for an action against banks invested in fossil fuels, we map the route of offices, wending through the financial district, churning high-rises. Scarlet pen slashes the paper like a fish tail cuts through foam.

In other words, to crescendo past the parameters of normalcy, to watch the river carry one's desires out, and out, beyond touch.

Desire: a process of resonance. A palm skimming the inside of my thigh. Lychees peeled in porcelain bowls. Watering flowers on a grave, its soil falling open. Pigment shivering on the many tongues

of a paintbrush.

Three years in, I couldn't continue as a therapist. Those fifty-minute hours, compressed to a few inches, the screen's blue hinges. Voices acquired a lag, clauses cleaved one from another. Nouns diluted. And I, pretending not to have drowned in synonymous stories. So sure, then, of the need for a forged neutrality. A fantasy of distance. My outcast child parts, powerless to narrate their own alternate endings, suffocating in repetition.

During Hong Kong's 2019 uprisings, protestors adopted the slogan, Be Water. The air boiled hot as a pinched nerve. Beneath tear gas, rubber bullets lapping at their skin. Power is so monotonous. How will we breathe in the future?

Lungs woozy, as they are, with wildfire, and virus-scarred. Two packs a day my father smoked, when I was a child. Every night, my airway narrowed with nightmares, until I threw up.

Check the air quality, we begin our sentences now. The sky saturated in some uncommon hue.

Yet, to imagine a self—familiar with impediment, yes, and riddled with shame—who might survive inside that chromatic future, its banality of fire, flood, and storm.

Consider also my friends, raising their first child. Cooking rice. Letting them pick out their own socks. Rinsing them in attention's most harmonic light. Yielding, and without resentment. Some fossilized image of childhood, rupturing inside me.

Though how might one make a life, should they inherit only the memory of silences, and blues, and much they would not have chosen to?

If I have a child, they will have survived my life, my mother's.

Before I was born, I was inoculated to water, the sonorous tide of my mother's life, breath humming through fluid and skin, and the world was all touch, and vibrations receding from a shore.

And water's incessant thrum, through ocean and rain and cloud and pond and sea and swamp and stream and creek and fog and lake and sound and mist, in and out of each other's bodies.

Faces brightened not by fish scale, or tear gas, or fever, but by laughter, its diatonic river.

If I may think of the future, my future, our futures, not as a threat of absence, but a change of form.

LIBERATION IS FOR THOSE WHO TREMBLE

after Cole Arthur Riley

whose breath weaves a mutiny
whose classrooms screen

armed struggle. who chews fury
sings strategy in every now. the weapon arteries

shut down, time sheets deserted, teeth
dislodged from duty

to the bottom line of billionaires. to die
is the burden of the living

the hours of mourning, multiplied
beyond feeling. my friends become comrades

in the streets. muscle of placards, call
and response. condemn the podiums and tear gas

the missile casings signed by children. the air burns
white and there is no innocence. first frost

overnight—the linden, the lilac
turned gold. I wake to a tall light

the dialectic of *I am afraid* and *do it*
anyway a tactile refrain

sediment of arms linked and debriefs
at the dive bar after arrest. in each reprisal

a fragment of home. grief sounded so loud
the glassed offices shatter with everyone inside

who was responsible. a dream is
a figment of sky. tonight, the I is full of kites

Being present to the struggle without trying to reduce the struggle into uncontainable objects means understanding that all of this is wild. Most of this is going to be violent. Even if we're pacifist, this state is not. Any opposition or threat to it will be disciplined in some way.

JOY JAMES, *IN PURSUIT OF REVOLUTIONARY LOVE*

Fascism has established itself in a most disguised and efficient manner in this country. It feels so secure that the leaders allow us the luxury of faint protest. Take protest too far, however, and they will show their other face. Doors will be kicked down in the night and machine-gun fire and buckshot will become the medium of exchange.

GEORGE JACKSON, *BLOOD IN MY EYE*

TPS, KKK, IOF YOU'RE ALL THE SAME

Once or twice a week, my mother messages me good morning, good afternoon, where the hell are you, or good evening. Children's medical play sets haven't changed in two decades:

stylish zipper carrying bag, weird little stethoscope, reflex hammer, plastic Band-Aid, thermometer, received ideas of class mobility and health. Stephen Harper spends $57,000

on an artificial lake outside the G20 Experience Canada pavilion, which cost $1.9 million. My mother's parents reside at the top of a windowless staircase in Kwun Tong.

My father delivers dessert to them on Saturdays. To enter, he recalls numbers into a keypad, drags an iron grate door. On Sundays, my mother helps him study. On Mondays, he

asks her to marry him. On the counter, he lines up the plastic vessels: sesame soup, almond soup, green bean, red. sixty years later, here I am. Upside down on monkey bars, knees shining the pipe, paint flaking off on my shins. Stones pave the path between the original playground and the parking lot that's replaced it. Each one a historical ache. Heavy in the stomach,

and rounded. A street medic collective, defunct since the 1990s, resurrects to support G20 counter organizing. Narrative exceeds the idea of childhood. I exert language as a

tactic. Posture from which I exercise control. Pen with which I excise containment. The cops peel off their name tags before using tear gas. The largest mass arrest in this settler

state's history. An incomplete list of complaints: lack of housing, stolen land, tar sands and deforestation, Israel's Gaza blockade, the summit's security costs. During the

Japanese occupation of Hong Kong, my mom and her sisters track dirt on their jaws and recite disappearance. I am a boy, I am a boy. My father feeds me rectangles of meat packed in

Styrofoam. No vegetables. A meal he couldn't have afforded in his own childhood. My mother is dead. Red-stained, the absence between grains of rice. White tablecloth over

the table, plastic dripping onto plastic chairs. Training as a medic, I practice first aid. Fake blood acquires colour from Red 40 and cocoa powder. Hue of torn fabric, envy, hospitals. To

achieve the right viscosity, we use corn syrup and icing sugar, much more than one would think. Plastic tubing threaded through green foam blocks. Pinch just the right place and

the bleeding stops. Late spring, we lock arms against a row of riot gear, behind us a three-dollar-sign Japanese resto-lounge in Yorkville. There are many more of us than them. Inside, a

Liberal MP poses with patrons. The MP votes to send weapons to Israel. The patrons touch palms over torched salmon, compressed stone fruit, wagyu wrapped in lettuce. Harper

says, *This is a classic attempt for us to be able to market the country.* Anarchists who firebombed a bank in Ottawa say, We'll be back. I pick my skin when I can't stop thinking.

Anxious, my fingers rip apart my lining. What sound does an arrest make when it doesn't happen? What sound does memory make when it swallows? To learn all possible tactics

to stop arrest or deportation: to surround the van, subtend the van, debase the van, defile the van, destroy the van, so it can't drive away. To analyze the conditions, one must

harden from surprise into suspicion. A wound furnishes a hole to be packed. Gauze unfurled on the laminate like a flag. Who fills an empty room with meaning? Who flushes tear gas from

the sidewalk? How many of us would it take to kettle a cop? G20 arrestees bring a class action lawsuit against the Toronto Police. Strangers become a state-sanctioned family. The lawyers

lust after their fees, $3 million. The Crown lusts after its legal definitions. When I am twelve, my brother chases me down a stony path. I fall. I bleed. I swipe my knees with alcohol.

Open air turned my insides from blue to red. For decades, my grandfather played chess against himself, his movements transcribed in scratches on the board. I learned to play

mahjong when my aunts lacked a fourth. They never taught me to keep score. We ate jarred jellies, roasted peanuts. A family is a liability, a futility. A distance impossible to cross

via effort. I don't always say what I mean, whether in English or Cantonese. A family is a problem of syntax, not vocabulary. Not knowing the rules forecloses the possibility of

winning. Still, I laid the squares of green bone on red felt. Tile by tile, word by word. A kettle is a panic room, a livestock enclosure, a door dipped in clay, the concept of Canada

whistling toward your face. A wound should be cleaned not with ethanol, but water. Tear gas should not be flushed from the eyes with milk, despite what some people say. Mail order medical supplies carry names like medieval pets: abdo pad, Transpore, arnica, tourniquet. Incomplete list of protest bans: the railroad blockade, the encampment

clearing, the highway overpass. In preparation for the G20, the TPS purchased four sound cannons. Milk is a process inside of the body. A blender spins sugar into blood, spills

red all over the kitchen counter. The Chinese character for mouth is a square. A square can be used as an enclosure. A kettle wrapped around another. Two nested mouths means

return. Three means you never attended Chinese school, your parents didn't care. My phone screen lights up: flying to Hong Kong tomorrow for a month. No need to reach

me. Regards, Dad. The Toronto police board agrees to a settlement of $16.5 million at the conclusion of the lawsuit. The 2025 city budget proposes a $46.2 million increase to the TPS, with little debate at the committee meeting. To render the present the same as the past: numbers depersonalize, depress the tongue. Open wide: a self spun inside

the machine called language, then laid flat to dry. Whatever a cop says to you, they're lying. Tear gas doesn't taste or smell like anything. Not ash, not exhaust, not white pepper, not

cuticle, not watermelon frost, not sesame seed pounded by stone or by hand. Fake blood resembles hot chocolate, then ketchup, poured into squeeze bottles for eye flush skill

stations. A child chases the aftermath around the kitchen, sugar dripping profligate from their mouth. The class action lawsuit settlement agreement states: *In considering standards for*

policing at future large scale events where public protest is anticipated, the Toronto Police Service ("TPS") has considered lessons learned from its experiences to date including the

June 2010 G20 Summit event held in downtown Toronto. Medics practice tactical neutrality. We pack white gauze into green foam. We pour red into the metal mouth where water

goes. As a child, on days I ate sugar, I had an asthma attack. Lungs yielding to dissident logic, refusing to labour. Sugar's arsenal: to appease, to asphyxiate. Sugar heats molten,

adheres to the skin, which makes sugar burns especially painful. Alone, I rehearsed dissolution, nightly heaving in the toilet, trying not to wheeze too loudly and wake my

father up. I am a boy, I am a boy, I am a boy. A non-linear trajectory of adolescence: compliance, disobedience, punishment. What sound does a square sing when it

closes? What compels the mind's door to unlock? If Marx says, not them. Mao says, why not. If a cop took my phone they could read my family's messages, the ones it takes me weeks to answer. Inflammation supports healing because it amplifies sensation, cleaves to the origin of pain. At the heritage cinema the film clicks forward, one square at a time. Despite

discomfort, an injured joint must move to recover. Movement is an illusion of interrupted light. A class action lawsuit is a rusted claw game, a hangnail of history, a hapless teacher

using a torn transparency to block the projector's light. Behind the playground there is a field and in the empty square there is a child and in the shut fist there is an inhaler and a

knife. There is no such thing as a good family, only a stone bleeding water. The walls of the house stumble closer, then closer. I remove my metals for the MRI. I have mistaken a

family for a sky. I have stumbled on syllables. I have, allegedly, lied to a cop. The difference between blood and water is the consequence of rupture. The difference between bone and plastic is weight, handfeel, the profusion of pores. Containment and care not as paired antagonism, but blended state. Anti-inflammatories ruin stomach lining. A wound

seals itself, one cell at a time.

MY MOTHER HAUNTS MY SATURN RETURN

no, not like memory. I was too young. more
like akebia grabbing the gutter and clothing
donations and churning lungs. after death

a home turns into cardboard boxes. blurry
from sleep, I pack the car. no, it was

my father. was it
a dream? I couldn't bloom fast enough

he couldn't drive at all. no, in my body's
language: electric green, sternum tingle

hummingbird in the nose. she's been dead
for years and finally I know

how to say it. according to astrologers
I've passed my first return. how vigorous
the vines spread, but I can trim them

myself. overnight, my grief grows
round and soft as a turnip
the future

hangs from me like a stone. no, not like
a plum. like an animal plummets from

a cliff, following the others. no, not
like a suicide. there is nothing

like a suicide. my father and I
keep trailing the same shadow

this year, the weather is warm
and terrifying. I blink and my life

passes through me. silver
blossoms explode in my hair

AGAINST THE COUPLE-FORM

after Clémence x. Clémentine

I expected digital lavender, noise
without faces. imagining a future
versus clinging to one. I've learned
there is a difference. the train running
late, my phone an archive of apologies
for absence. I miss you. have you been
kind to yourself today. happiness was simple
and perilous. a pear tree, a protest, a fistful
of pages. I filled the margins with verbs.
yield. invert. infect. syllables invented
to describe how you changed me, as when
I practiced refusing. no, I will not pay
for entry. I will let love get involved.
desire is stateless, but distance was
always laughing. how long the wait,
and abject, I waited. we only came
when we were touching ourselves.

MOVEMENT V

[audio score:

on its own the organ cannot sound, only
touch activates song. touch I hear from beginning
to end, long tones integrate attention and silence.
add chime and scrape, luminous, spare, like stars
disturbing the lambent sky with their precision.
triangle the brightest shape. between duration
                                    and memory, pearl barley
                                                                        falls from glass to glass.

at the bookstore in Sham Shui Po I read a sticker:
if you're going to be armed, be self-reflective.

echoes stir across the ear. language pushes
meaning through the mind, which is a membrane

enfolding and inside of time. brushstrokes
of ink, drying on rice paper. glass scattering

light. my lover says: I'm sorry,
I had to make you something beautiful.

rain, through the roof of the former arms factory.

postmemory is proof of species-being.
the wind of a stranger, passing by.

the sound of water on rocks, of conviction
on pavement, of many—passing through.]

What does it mean for us to enact madness, to animate madness, to animate refusals, to animate life, to animate choosing our comrades?

DR. IDIL ABDILLAHI, "DECARCERATING CARE: THE PATHOLOGIZING OF RESISTANCE"

AGAIN, NOSTALGIA

sometimes the past depends on the future and what
it illuminates. expectations and exits. the difference

between psychoanalytic and political resistance
is the direction of the door. you are as young as you'll ever
be again, as unencumbered. you purchased tickets

to the wedding of disparate nostalgias. you
reclined in the plush, state-sponsored seats.
for a moment, unforgivably, wrong was elsewhere.

property language is passé in relation to love.
the poem wants to convey this, but can't—

the abject failure of logic to circumvent desire.
how your lover's hand feels under your skirt

in the dark. with every touch there was
the tang of white pepper, the tightening
of prayer, your tongue quiet and quickened

until the littlest hours. the hinge swings
inward. history slips out. light rising
from light. linen bedsheets in the mirror.

none of this is or will be yours.
in the past, you would have made promise

after promise to keep it, though
surveilled, though aggrieved, though longing

to give your time not to love, but liberation.

now you want to be a dictionary of air.

you want to be the language
their life passes through, then leaves.

AGAINST THE HURRICANE

You search for plausible reasons to have enrolled in the wilderness first aid course, describing your interest as personal, not professional. The boy beside you, with decades of camp counsellor inside him, invites you on a four-day canoeing trip. You do not camp. You don't tell him you've never fixed a tent to soil on your own, nor lifted a bear canister into branches with synthetic rope.

Wilderness medicine traces its roots to the military. Early navy surgeons treated wounds in remote environments. Before signing up, you scrolled the list of potential trainers: ex-cop, paramedic, ex-soldier, ex-cop. Your eyes moved quickly, listening closely. Their headshots disclosed the shoulders of their uniforms, regardless of how long since they left active duty. To pass a course, one must be able to read and follow orders.

Four years before that room, therapy school impelled each student to disclose their inciting wounds. You refused to play. Extractions, estrangements. Citing theories on PTSD, you watched hardship confer upon your classmates the moral authority to mistreat each other. Appealing for care as a familiar posture. Triggers competing in a downward spiral of bad behaviour.

In an article on the history of Médecins sans frontières (MSF), Mary Turfah cautions: *The limits of listening to the body, as medics are trained to do, is that the body can't tell you that genocide suits American foreign interests.* Canadian interests, too. It's so Canadian for commercially successful authors to render the colonized not as collective subjects, but traumatized objects. It's so Canadian to write one's hands off the drone, the trigger, the agentic threat. MSF's first warzone trip was made to Beirut in 1976, following Zionist Phalangists' attack on a bus of Palestinians. *The New York Times* described the incident as a justified attack on militants. In 2025, Writers Against the War on Gaza launched a boycott campaign against *The New York Times*. MSF refused to identify Israel's occupation as the original crime. Their volunteers treated "both sides."

Political lineage is a fixture of your street medic education, which you pursue in parallel to therapy and first aid. In 1970, Black Panthers and Young Lords occupied Lincoln Hospital and developed the first acupuncture detox clinic, offering community medicine and classes in Marxism. Free treatment as a communist offensive. Dual power: a strategy in which a party-like structure confronts the state while building alternatives to provide for the needs of the people. You learn how to offer care in proportion to your capabilities. At the Palestine solidarity student encampment, patrolling the tent circle, distributing granola bars sunscreen aloe bottled water—you remember there are people who want each other to live.

And yet:

> The masses are not ready for more militant action.
> The conditions are not ripe for guerrilla warfare.
> Collective healing is antagonistic to violence.
> We must meet the people where they're at.

Inside yourself, you make excuses for what you fear.
You repress every fresh whisper of it.

You did not occupy any negligent hospital nor corporate media headquarters. You did not burn the newspapers which, with their sanctioned words, lent legitimacy to the public image of a genocide. You did not divulge the university president's home address. You did not seize survival supplies made illicit. You wore a hoodie with a graphic of a cop car on fire. You did not stink bomb the legislature. You posed for photographs in marbled lobbies. You despise the phrase, moving at the pace of trust. There's always a reason not to do something. There's always a reason not to trust.

Fifty years have passed since George Jackson wrote: *We are faced with two choices: to continue as we have done for forty years fanning our pamphlets against the hurricane, or starting to build a new revolutionary culture that we will be able to turn on the old culture.*

To certify as wilderness medics, you and your fellow trainees practice each skill to basic competence, alternating turns as patients. You animate a fake asthma attack with your body which is prone, often, to real asthma attacks. The instructor praises your acting, picks you out as a patient for the final test. Proud of your talent as an object, and poor in oxygen, you retrieve your inhaler from your bag. In almost half of all adult CPR cases, the ribcage cracks to accommodate breath. The shoulder blades protect the lungs indirectly. Yours, full of arthritis, hurt more than they help.

The culminating scenario is set at an imaginary lake after a thunderstorm. There are three patients, nine rescuers, the pressures of diminishing time and external evaluation. In the wilderness, your trainer says, chaos produces crisis. One patient, struck by lightning, bleeds from their eardrums. Your case presents as less severe—a fall down a hill, worry for your friends—but if your rescuers move you without a proper assessment, your wounded spine will swell, forecasting nerve damage. A third patient, impaled by a tree, is marked for imminent death. To succeed, the rescuers must ration their attention, allot their time to the appropriate victims. They leave you on the ground for last, as they are meant to. Your pain, accurately counted, falls short of the threshold for care.

By the time he resigned from Blida-Joinville, Fanon regretted attenuating the pain of colonizing soldiers. One case involved a French policeman in an anti-FLN brigade. We have to go through with it, the policeman said, describing a beating. He taxonomized screams according to the stage of interrogation. He started to hear the screams everywhere. Another officer begged Fanon to cure his nightmares; to help him go on torturing Algerians.

Trauma shows you a person folding inward, Turfah writes, *shearing their tether to the world. Trauma cannot get one to struggle, in the sense of committing to something bigger than their person—a cause—because it only recognizes a world mediated by individual human bodies . . . Trauma narratives absent political valences offered the possibility of parity: occupiers suffer too. Personal testimonies are raw material, malleable and manipulated by political actors to serve various ends.*

The psychiatrists you know wouldn't call themselves militants. They sign forms and present diagnoses. They attend the protests in their spare time. For allegedly robbing a Brink's truck in 1981, Mutulu Shakur—Lincoln Detox acupuncturist, political education instructor, and assistant program director— was sentenced to sixty years in prison. two hundred NYPD officers, under direction of Ed Koch, shut down the clinic in 1978.

The state's greatest weapon is fear. Street medics don't treat cops or their supporters. You ask yourself: What are you willing to do? What are you not willing to do? What risks do you limit? What limits can you risk?

At the fake lake, no one assesses you for spinal injury. No one presses a needle to the back of your hands. Left hand or right hand? Sharp or dull? Is it too late to form a clandestine affinity group? Is it too late to scrub your name from the internet? To triage for survival is to make a contaminated decision. The fictional bruise on your vertebrae escapes detection. When you scream in pain, you convince even yourself.

Your trainer prompts you to offer feedback, but your rescuer doesn't want to know what he forgot. With his toe, he scuffs the dirt; his shame neutralizes your critique. Both of you pass the training. Three months later, police pepper-spray your friends during a jail support rally. The water you pour over their eyes and hands runs into the gutter. Riding the subway home, you rip the red tape on your backpack denoting your role as a medic. Your exterior, bare and unmarked, gives nothing away.

CENTO WITH THE WATERS RISING

at the end of the world, let there be you
saint of the blue peaks by the ocean where we began

a trail of hands
narrating in the context of ache, or, tomorrow
crowned with August and salt

the way old grief is gentle
I wake in a puddle of ghost
I hunt the wilderness in myself

these ever-blooming wounds
rustle nude inside the blue water

to answer your question: I refuse

history is a song
new name for a myth already lived in

the thought of losing sight of shore
you know, no one can prepare for

hair falling in torrents, roses
of lips, the plummeted paper
planes, the angry weather

there is no prayer or pill for this

alive means you swallow
each day like a stone

I, too, am built out of a question about the sky

if language can hybrida, anemone, ever be enough
to repair, begin again

where everything you've lost is washed ashore
I'm building the boat—I believe
I exist, a historian of my own silence

think of a needle dropped into the sea
the moon, a wound

on the lake, our footprints
to not follow

if you don't have blood on your hands
by the end of this you weren't listening

inside every world there is another
world trying to get out—

my marigold my wave
sun-glass breaking

like the light I am scattered
& what is left is only water

REFERENCES

Clémence x. Clémentine, "Suturing the Split: Coda on the Couple-Form" (*GUTS*, 2016)

Cynthia Cruz, "Notes Toward a New Language: On La Borde" (*Poetry Foundation*, 2015)

Frantz Fanon, *The Psychiatric Writings from Alienation and Freedom* (Bloomsbury, 2020), *Toward the African Revolution* (Monthly Review Press, 1967), and *The Wretched of the Earth* (Grove Press, 2021)

aracelis girmay, *the black maria* (BOA Editions, Ltd., 2016) and "The PEN Ten: An Interview with aracelis girmay" (PEN America, 2023)

Félix Guattari, *Chaosophy: Texts and Interviews 1972–1977* (Semiotext(e), 2008)

Alexis Pauline Gumbs, *Undrowned: Black Feminist Lessons from Marine Mammals* (AK Press, 2020)

George Jackson, *Blood in My Eye* (Black Classic Press, 1990)

Joy James, *In Pursuit of Revolutionary Love* (Divided Publishing, 2022)

Taylor Johnson, *Inheritance* (Alice James Books, 2020)

Fred Moten and Stefano Harney, *The Undercommons: Fugitive Planning & Black Study* (Minor Compositions, 2013)

Bahar Orang, *Where Things Touch* (Book*hug Press, 2020)

Jamila Osman, "the guerrilla is like a poet" (*Medium*, 2024)

Leah Lakshmi Piepzna-Samarasinha, *The Future Is Disabled* (Arsenal Pulp Press, 2022)

Dylan Robinson, *Hungry Listening: Resonant Theory for Indigenous Sound Studies* (University of Minnesota Press, 2020)

Jane Shi, "Reimagining the Autistic Mother Tongue" (Disability Visibility Project, 2021)

François Tosquelles, "A Politics of Madness" (*Parapraxis Magazine*, 2024)

Mary Turfah, "Doctors Without Politics" (*The Baffler*, 2025)
Sasha Warren, *Storming Bedlam: Madness, Utopia, and Revolt* (Common Notions, 2024)
Deborah Wong, *Louder and Faster: Pain, Joy, and the Body Politic in Asian American Taiko* (University of California Press, 2019)
shō yamagushiku, "we are rejoicing as japanese america is falling into dust" (*SYGYZY*, 2025)

ECOSYSTEM (POETRY IS A COMMUNAL PRACTICE)

Beatrice Adler-Bolton and Artie Vierkant, *Health Communism* (Verso Books, 2022)
Etel Adnan, *The Arab Apocalypse* (The Post-Apollo Press, 2023)
Zaina Alsous, *A Theory of Birds* (University of Arkansas Press, 2019)
Tina Campt, *Listening to Images* (Duke University Press, 2017)
Aimé Cesaire, *Discourse on Colonialism* (Monthly Review Press, 2000)
Raven Chacon, *For Zitkála-Šá* (Art Metropole, 2022)
JJJJJerome Ellis, *The Clearing* (Wendy's Subway, 2021)
Ruth Wilson Gilmore, *Abolition Geography: Essays Towards Liberation* (Verso Books, 2022)
Sky Hopinka, *Jáaji Approx.* (2015)
June Jordan, *Some of Us Did Not Die: Selected Essays* (Basic/Civitas Books, 2002)
Robin D. G. Kelley, Freedom Dreams: *The Black Radical Imagination* (Beacon Press, 2002)
Tanya Lukin Linklater, *Slow Scrape* (Talonbooks, 2022)
Pauline Oliveros, *Deep Listening: A Composer's Sound Practice* (Deep Listening Publications, 2005)
M. NourbeSe Philip, "Interview with an Empire" (*Lemon Hound*, 2017)
Solmaz Sharif, *Customs* (Graywolf Press, 2022)
Jane Shi, *echolalia echolalia* (Brick Books, 2024)
Eric A. Stanley, *Atmospheres of Violence: Structuring Antagonism and the Trans/Queer Ungovernable* (Duke University Press, 2021)
Fargo Nissim Tbkahi, *TERROR COUNTER* (Deep Vellum, 2025)

ACKNOWLEDGMENTS

I am indebted to those who have fought behind and against prison walls of all kinds, writing resistance with their bodies and minds, breaking open on the terrible world. to those whose madness multiplies struggle, whose demands the state cannot steal nor understand. this book is dedicated to you.

previous versions of some of these poems first appeared in the following publications: *A Body You Talk To: An Anthology on Contemporary Disability* (Sundress Publications, 2023), *Arc Poetry Magazine*, *EVENT*, *Midnight Sun*, *NightBlock*, *smoke and mold*, and *Seventh Wave*.

"cento with the waters rising" is composed entirely of lines borrowed from: "acknowledgments" by Danez Smith, "when they ask me who i pray to" by Jess Rizkallah, "poem in which I" by Eunice Andrada, "you're so paranoid" by Franny Choi, "Untitled" by Rachel McKibbens, "enough food and a mom" by francine j. harris, "Malinche" by Vanessa Angélica Villarreal, "Postcolonial Love Poem" by Natalie Diaz, "Dream Diary" by Yanyi, "bird survives the death of Nature" by Zaina Alsous, "Canadian Sonnet" by Billy-Ray Belcourt, "Abecedarian Requiring Further Examination Before a Diagnosis Can Be Determined" by torrin a. greathouse, "Labanotation 31" by Esther Lee, "Shahr-e-janaan: The city of the beloved" by Adeeba Shahid Talukder, "Come" by Gillian Sze, "Letter From My Heart to My Brain / Letter From My Brain To My Heart" by Rachel McKibbens, "Commandments" by Donika Kelly, *The Black Maria* by aracelis girmay, "Reading Darwish in Vermont" by Zaina Alsous, "All my friends are sad & bright" by Cameron Awkward-Rich, "Trans is Against Nostalgia" by Taylor Johnson, "I Believe I Exist" by Billy-Ray Belcourt, "Broken Heart Emoji,

Crystal Ball Emoji, Stars Emoji" by Kyla Jamieson, "Human Interest Story" by Sandra Lim, "Tankas" by Victoria Chang, "Mind Over Matter" by Shira Erlichman, "Amor Fati" by Sandra Lim, "Aubade" by Taylor Johnson, and "self-portrait with lake nasser" by Safia Elhillo.

all my gratitude to Alayna Munce and Manahil Bandukwala for making poetry material with the utmost care, to Cecily Nicholson for sharpening the ethic and spirit of these poems, to Myung-Sun Kim for the blue insides, to Michael DeForge for the blue outsides, to Yang Chen for the sound of madness, and to Mercedes Eng, Rob Macaisa Colgate, Thea Lim, and Gabrielle Bates for the words of support.

this book would not exist without the company and labour of many friends and comrades, including: Adrienne, Aliya, Amy, Anna, Bahar, CeCe, Cricket, Elizabeth, Fan, Fathima, Furqan, Jane, Janika, Kris, Lorraine, Maysam, Michael, Noa, Norm, Sallie, Sanna, Sheung-King, Thea, Yang, Zoë. may movement be our continued horizon, our togetherness as long as our commitment.

Jody Chan is a poet, multidisciplinary artist, care worker, and community organizer based in Toronto. They are the author of two previous books of poetry: *sick* (Black Lawrence Press, 2020), finalist for the Lambda Literary and Pat Lowther Memorial Awards, and winner of the 2018 St. Lawrence Book Award and 2021 Trillium Award for Poetry; and *impact statement* (Brick Books, 2024), longlisted for the Pat Lowther Memorial Award. Jody was the 2023-2024 Artist-in-Residence at the University of Toronto's Queer and Trans Research Lab, and the 2023 recipient of the Joseph S. Stauffer Prize in Literature from the Canada Council for the Arts.

Achevé d'imprimer
sur les presses de l'imprimerie Gauvin,
Gatineau, Québec, Canada